ASK
ABOUT

ASIA

Mason Crest Publishers Inc.
370 Reed Road
Broomall, Pennsylvania 19008
(866) MCP-BOOK (toll free)

First printing

1 2 3 4 5 6 7 8 9 10

Library of Congress Cataloging-in-Publication Data on file at the
Library of Congress.

ISBN 1-59084-205-7
ISBN 1-59084-198-0 (series)

Printed in Malaysia.

Adapted from original concept produced by
Vineyard Freepress Pty Ltd, Sydney.
Copyright © 2002 Vineyard Freepress Pty Ltd.

Project Editor and Text: Valerie Hill
Design Production: Fiona Kirkman
Consultant: Joan Grant
Cartography: Peter Barker
Prepress: Dein Miskell
Printer: Toppan Printing
Images: Tourism Authority of Thailand, Margaret Sams, Royal Thai
Consulate, Thai Airways International, Peter Barker, Samsam, Christa
Sams, Wayne Morton, Australian War Memorial Museum, David
Jones, Allen Roberts, Bibliotheque Francais, Oxford University Press.

COVER: Traditional *khon* dance.

TITLE PAGE: Royal palace decoration.

CONTENTS: Riverside dwellings in north Thailand.

INTRODUCTION: Hill tribe girls.

Thailand

MASON CREST PUBLISHERS

CONTENTS

THE LAND

PEOPLE AND NATION

SURROUNDED BY WARS

INTRODUCTION

THE KINGDOM OF THAILAND's early beginnings can be seen in the massive ruins of its first cities. The Buddhist way of life begun then is still followed by most Thais and the king remains their greatly honored head of state. Called the "land of the free," Thailand remained independent when other Southeast Asian countries were colonized.

Most people live in farming villages, growing abundant food for the nation and for export. Bangkok, the huge, hurrying capital, is a center of technology and a leading Southeast Asian trader in world markets. While becoming industrialized, Thailand is also aware of the need to conserve its beautiful mountains, forests, and rivers, long the habitats of some of the world's most exotic birds and animals.

▲ Forested mountains and rivers to the north.

▲ Three countries, Thailand, Laos, and Myanmar, meet at Thailand's northern tip. Here also, the great Mekong River can be seen.

▼ The tapir's black and white markings allow it to merge into patches of light and shade in the evergreen forests of the southwest.

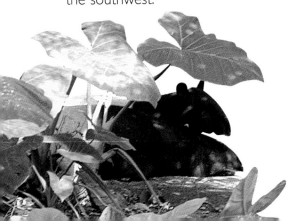

THAILAND— HEART OF THE MAINLAND

Southeast Asia has two geographic regions: the mainland (a large peninsula off the Asian continent) and the maritime (or island) countries. Thailand is in the center of mainland Southeast Asia, which also includes Myanmar (Burma), Laos, Cambodia, Vietnam, and Malaysia. Thailand's north is forested and mountainous, with rivers running through deep valleys to a fertile central basin. To the northeast is the dry and harsh Khorat Plateau. Lower down, abundant rice is grown in the Chao Phraya River basin. The capital, Bangkok, is on the Chao Phraya river which runs into the Gulf of Thailand. The southern tip is on the narrow Malay Peninsula, a rain-forested mountain range between the Gulf and the Andaman Sea. Hundreds of islands dot the warm waters off the coastline.

CLIMATE

Seasons are set by monsoons, which bring rain, wind, and floods. In the tropical south, it rains all year round. Over the rest of the land monsoon rains are followed by a cooler season, then a hot, dry summer. Chiang Mai in the north has six dry months but Phuket in the south has only two. Temperatures vary from near-freezing in the north to 97.5°F (35°C) in the south.

▲ Tropical fish and coral off the Malay Peninsula.

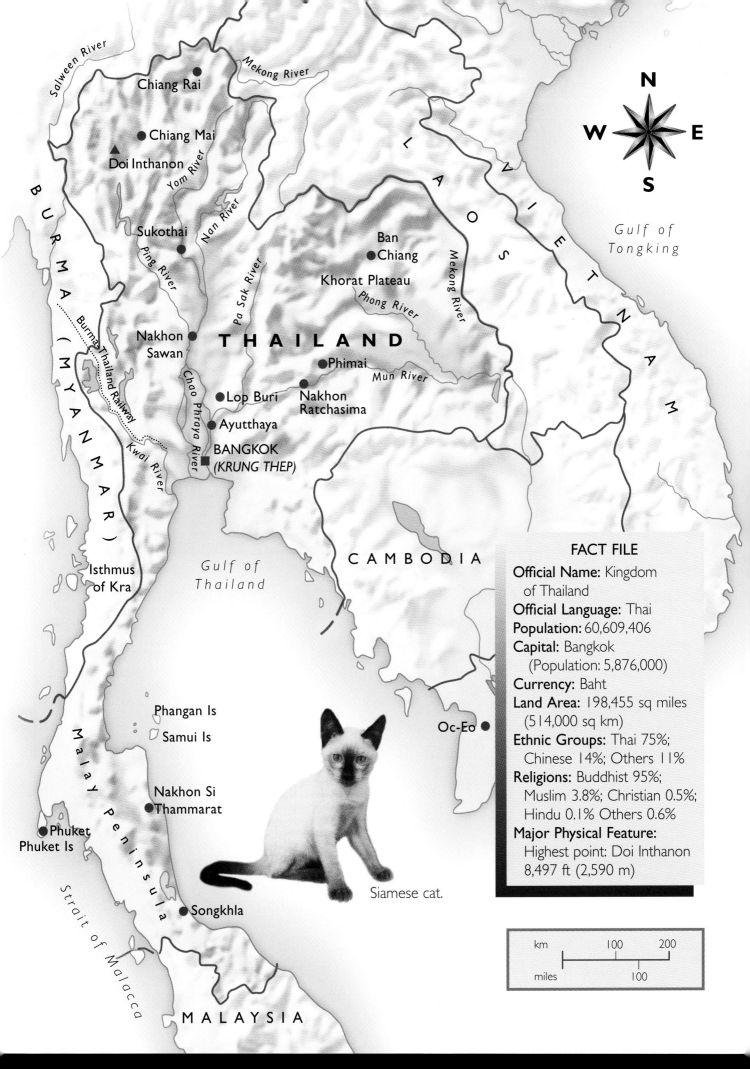

Salween River

Chiang Rai

Mekong River

Chiang Mai

Doi Inthanon

Yom River

Nan River

Sukothai

Ping River

BURMA (MYANMAR)

Burma–Thailand Railway

Pa Sak River

Nakhon Sawan

THAILAND

Kwai River

Chao Phraya River

Lop Buri

Ayutthaya

BANGKOK (KRUNG THEP)

Ban Chiang

Khorat Plateau

Phong River

Mekong River

Phimai

Mun River

Nakhon Ratchasima

LAOS

VIETNAM

Gulf of Tongking

N W E S

Isthmus of Kra

Gulf of Thailand

CAMBODIA

Oc-Eo

Phangan Is

Samui Is

Malay Peninsula

Nakhon Si Thammarat

Phuket
Phuket Is

Strait of Malacca

Songkhla

MALAYSIA

Siamese cat.

FACT FILE

Official Name: Kingdom of Thailand

Official Language: Thai

Population: 60,609,406

Capital: Bangkok (Population: 5,876,000)

Currency: Baht

Land Area: 198,455 sq miles (514,000 sq km)

Ethnic Groups: Thai 75%; Chinese 14%; Others 11%

Religions: Buddhist 95%; Muslim 3.8%; Christian 0.5%; Hindu 0.1% Others 0.6%

Major Physical Feature: Highest point: Doi Inthanon 8,497 ft (2,590 m)

km   100   200

miles   100

TRAVELERS OF GREAT NATURAL HIGHWAYS

The region occupied by Thailand was an ancient migration route. Over the centuries diverse peoples and animal species traveled from continental Asia down into this southeastern peninsula, where they spread out or gradually moved on to the islands beyond. The natural "highways" they followed were not roads as we know them, but rivers. These rivers made it possible to travel through the wild, almost-impassable mountains and down to the lower fertile basins and deltas. Beginning in the great Himalayas, ranges and rivers run from north to south, radiating like the arms of an octopus through the peninsula. Many of the peoples and animals moving along these natural routes made Thailand their home.

MOUNTAIN, RIVER, AND MONSOON "HIGHWAYS" OF MAINLAND SOUTHEAST ASIA

GREAT MOUNTAIN RANGES
running north to south (green arrows)

DAWNA-TENASSERIM RANGES stretch from eastern Tibet to the Malay Peninsula

ARAKAN-YOMA RANGES divide India and Burma (Myanmar)

ANNAMITE RANGE divides Laos and Vietnam

▼ The *Akha* tribes began to migrate from Tibet 2,000 years ago, and now move between China, Myanmar, and Thailand (the only country that does not harrass them).

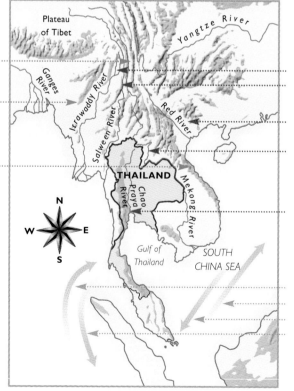

GREAT RIVERS
running from north to south (blue arrows)

IRRAWADDY RIVER and SALWEEN RIVER, Burma (Myanmar)

RED RIVER, Vietnam

MEKONG RIVER flows from Tibet to the South China Sea

CHAO PHRAYA RIVER, Thailand's major waterway

MONSOON WINDS
(grey arrows) blow southwest from May to mid-September and northeast from December

(Map labels: Plateau of Tibet, Yangtze River, Ganges River, Irrawaddy River, Salween River, Red River, THAILAND, Chao Praya River, Mekong River, Gulf of Thailand, SOUTH CHINA SEA, N, S, E, W)

Dinosaur fossils are found in Thailand's northeast region. A set of footprints, each measuring over 10 feet (3 meters) long, show that the meat-eating Allosaurus once strode about this part of Thailand. The plant-eating Sauropod also inhabited this area.

Sun bears are at home in the crags of Khao Sok Park in the Malayan Peninsula.

Some of the most exotic animals in the world lived in the ideal habitats of the peninsula. Myriad plants thrived, providing food and shelter for great Asian elephants and tigers, rhinoceros, crocodiles, deer, and tiny creatures, and for some 925 bird species (more than exist in all of Europe). Now, most of these animals and many birds are extinct or threatened by over-hunting and clearing of forests for timber and cultivation. Many of the remaining animals live in national parks or are domesticated.

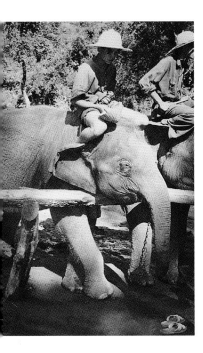

These young Asian elephants work and play with their *mahouts* (trainers). Many *mahouts* are Karens, the earliest and largest tribe to migrate to the peninsula from a Chinese-Tibetan region. Now they live in a small area on Thailand's west border (see the map on page 15). A beautiful Thai film, *The Elephant Keeper,* shows how people, elephants, and forests depend on one another.

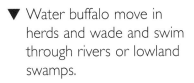

◀ Red pandas move about in treetops or on the ground.

▼ Water buffalo move in herds and wade and swim through rivers or lowland swamps.

▶ Sunbirds live in the cool forests of Doi Ithanon, Thailand's highest mountain.

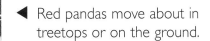

PEOPLES OF FOREST AND RIVER

Bronze musical instruments, jewelry, and pottery urns were made and used by Thailand's earliest inhabitants as far back as 4000 BC. Much later, about 200 BC, these earliest people were joined by tribes driven from southern China by war and other disasters. Some of them, the *Kon Pa,* or "people of the forest," hunted wild animals and grew vegetables and rice in the mountains. But the *Kon Muang,* or "people of the town," went further south to the river basins, where they had both water to grow rice and summers hot and dry enough to ripen the grain. Here they were able to feed large populations and build powerful civilizations. The Kon Muang crafted metal tools and pottery and harvested salt, which they exchanged with the Kon Pa for things gathered from the forest, such as honey, resins, wild animal skins, ivory, and herbs.

▲
Wet rice, irrigated with river water, has provided food since early settlement. Grains found in clay pots at Ban Chiang show that rice was grown there about 6,000 years ago (4000 BC).

▲▶
Rice-growers painted the things they saw along the Mekong River: giant catfish (still found in the river), a soft-shelled turtle, and men with fish traps. Red paint, mixed from soil, fat, and tree gum, was used to paint a mural on rockface near Pha Taem. It measures 560 feet (170 meters) long and is over 2,000 years old.

◀ Bronze musical instruments played about 2700 BC at Ban Chiang. Some of the earliest bronzework in the world has been found in Thailand.

▶ A shepherd boy, falling into a hole near Ban Chiang, found hundreds of ancient clay pots, the earliest fired earthen-ware in South-east Asia.

The skills and crafts of early forest-dwellers have been passed down through many generations. The Akha people, for example, who live in remote mountain villages, rely on the forest for much of their daily needs and the women still weave and sew in the traditional way.

Ton Khram

▲ Keeping their traditional skills, the Akha thatch roofs and weave baskets from grasses and leaves.

▲ Cotton for weaving is hung in bundles to dry after being dyed. The indigo-blue dye is made from the *Ton Khram* plant.

▼ This thatched house, with its earth floor and sleeping platform, is built high on a mountain side, where the Akha always live.

▲ This woven *ikat* pattern is derived from trees and snakes (*nagas*). Traditional tribal art was not just for decoration. Its symbols were intended to invoke magical powers to protect people and crops.

▲ Akha women embroider clothing and the headdress, which they wear all day.

▶ Fowls have pecked around village houses for unknown ages. This cheeky little Bantam rooster is descended from the Thai native red jungle fowl.

A JIGSAW OF LANGUAGES

▲
These girls speak the dialect of their village at Thailand's northern tip.

Many different peoples make up the Thai nation of today. Most of them came to Thailand during the last six hundred years, but some have lived in the region for thousands of years. In their speech there are clues to their past: where they came from, who they are related to, and what they believe. Eighty percent of the population speak Thai, the national language, but many small local communities use different dialects (they add words or say them in their own way). Also, many of the Hill Tribes speak their own ancient languages. In addition, they learn Thai at school, through television and magazines, and as they trade or work in cities.

My child hears words and learns meanings from me and also from those around him. When he grows up he will pass our language and customs on to his children.

PASSING ON LANGUAGE BY SPEAKING

Many Hill Tribes have no written language—their language, history, and culture are passed on by everyday speech, stories, traditions, and rituals. Tribes who have only an oral (spoken) history include the Karen (see pink on the language map).

PASSING ON WAYS OF WRITING A LANGUAGE

Before writing a language there has to be an alphabet. Most nations adapt one already in use. The Thai alphabet was adapted about 700 years ago from Mon and Khmer (still spoken in areas colored green on the language map). And their system of writing had come much earlier from India's ancient Sanskrit, one of the oldest written languages.

SOUNDS AND TONES OF THE THAI LANGUAGE

▶ This letter of the Thai alphabet stands for the sound "ph" ("f") as in "phone."

▶ When speaking the Thai language the meaning of a word is altered by a change of tone. There are five different tones: low, middle, high, falling, and rising.

Try saying "mai" in five tones:

		FALLING
• HIGH	mai	ma͟i
• MIDDLE	mai	
• LOW	mai	ma͞i
		RISING

Thailand has many "language families" that are also found in other Southeast Asian countries. In the map below, different colors are used to show the jigsaw of languages. You can see that people from the same language family sometimes spread over large areas, while others live in small groups.

▶ The Tai Lue tribe migrated or were captured from Yunnan, China, and still live in the mountains and keep their Tai dress and language. The growth of the Thai nation is shown by the large Thai-speaking area in yellow on the map.

▲
The Yao tribe are Thai citizens who belong to the Miao-Yao language family (see aqua areas on map). They migrated from China and write their language, history, and business documents in Chinese.

SPELLING

• You will see two different spellings—T-a-i used here for tribes and language families—and T-h-a-i, a more modern spelling, as used in "Thailand." Both words mean "free" and come from the same roots.

• Changes in spelling occur in a living language as it is used and adapted.

• New words are added when people move, or borrow words from other languages, or when new things are invented (such as television or E-mail).

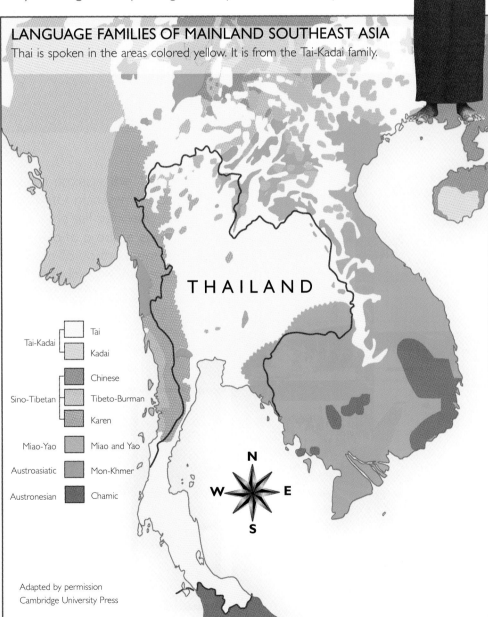

LANGUAGE FAMILIES OF MAINLAND SOUTHEAST ASIA
Thai is spoken in the areas colored yellow. It is from the Tai-Kadai family.

THAILAND

Tai-Kadai
- Tai
- Kadai

Sino-Tibetan
- Chinese
- Tibeto-Burman
- Karen

Miao-Yao
- Miao and Yao

Austroasiatic
- Mon-Khmer

Austronesian
- Chamic

Adapted by permission
Cambridge University Press

TRADERS, KINGS, & TEMPLES

Thailand has absorbed much Indian culture. Hinduism and Buddhism, writing, literature, and ideas about kingship and administration came quietly into the prosperous kingdoms of the peninsula as they traded with India from about AD 300. For example, Hindu temples were built by Indian seagoing traders in Oc-eo, the ancient capital of Funan. Oc-eo controlled the sea-lanes between India and China, because it had both a sheltered seaport and fertile lands for growing food for the ships' crews. From about AD 600 Indian culture also came to the north through overland trade routes to Dvaravati. And in the south it came through Srivijaya, part of the rich Hindu maritime empire of Sumatra, which extended along the Malay Peninsula. Gradually Indian culture was adapted to the Thai way of life.

▲ Indian trading ships sailed southwest with the monsoons to the Isthmus of Kra. There, cargo was carried overland to ships in the Gulf of Thailand. Traders waited at Oc-eo for up to five months until the northeast winds took them on to China or back to India.

▼ This modern ploughing ceremony is really a very old Brahman ritual. Brahmans (Indian scholars of Hindu religion and culture) were the teachers, scribes, and bookkeepers of the Thai court. They held high positions and directed court rituals and ceremonies, including the cremation of kings.

The Khmer Empire controlled a great part of present-day Thailand, Cambodia, and Laos. It was a Hindu civilization, famous for the ancient ruins of its capital, Angkor. In AD 802, Jayavarman II proclaimed himself ruler of all the Khmer people.

He, and kings after him, added to their names the suffix *-varman*, which means "armor" or "protector" of the people, the state, the soil, and especially the water. The Khmer Empire extended to Phimai until the Tai's persistent invasions overcame it in 1353.

▲ Commander of a Tai army.

▲ Children and adults perform an ancient Mon dance. The Mon people lived across the north of Thailand from the fifth century AD and founded the Dvarvarti kingdom in the Chao Phraya river valley.

► Silver Namo coins used in Srivijaya 8–13th century AD.

► Khmer alto fiddle (*saw-u*) made from wood, ivory, and a coconut shell covered with cowskin. The bow is used between the neck and the strings.

◄ The Khmers built this Hindu temple in the city of Lopburi. Later a statue of Buddha was placed in it.

► A snake-like creature called a *naga*, important in both Animist and Chinese beliefs, guards a temple of the Lan na Kingdom.

MIXING RELIGIONS TOGETHER

As armies, migrants, and travelers brought their beliefs with them, religions were mixed together, so that present-day Asian religions include ideas from Animism, Hinduism, Buddhism, Islam, and many sects and cults.

▲
In an elephant duel King Intradit, "Glorious Sun King," defeated the Khmers and in 1240 founded the Sukothai Kingdom. Many Mon and Khmers remained as his subjects.

COMING OF THE THAI

The Thai lived in southern China during the Tang Dynasty (AD 618–907). To escape the Chinese many moved south, where they accepted the culture of earlier peoples, such as the Mon and Khmer. The first Thai capital was Sukhothai (Sook-o-tie). When China was overrun by the Mongols in the 1250s more tribes fled south and set up small kingdoms. A strong leader, Mengrai, established Lan-na, "Kingdom of One Million Ricefields," and brought the small kingdoms together in the city of Chiang Mai in 1296. This date is celebrated as the birth of the modern nation. While the Thais called their country *Muang Thai*, "Land of the Free," it was widely known as Siam and the people as Siamese.

IN THE CITY OF SUKHOTHAI (1240–1365)

Monks from Ceylon introduced Theravada Buddhism and taught that good works would "gain merit" (credit points for after death). So, to gain great merit, Kings built the massive temples and statues that tower among the ruins of the ancient city of Sukhothai.

In 1283 an alphabet and system of writing was devised from Mon and Khmer script. It is still used to write the Thai language. The oldest example is King Ramkamhaeng's inscription: "Sukhothai is good. There are fish in the river, there is rice in the fields."

Cowrie shells were used as coins by Indian traders.

Sukhothai spent so much on its temples and court processions that it became weak and Ayutthaya became the capital. The city was built on an island at the confluence of three rivers; canals were its streets and houseboats were the people's homes. Located on the India-to-China trade route, Ayutthaya grew large and rich and was thronged with foreign traders from forty different nations. As travelers approached, their eyes were dazzled by the golden spires of temples. When they arrived, they could buy rice, spices, timber, and hides. Ayutthaya's 400-year golden age ended in 1767, when Burmese armies plundered and burned the city and its rice fields, and took tens of thousands of prisoners. A remnant of the Thai army continued to fight the Burmese and moved the capital to a safer place on the Chao Phraya River, where it has grown during the past 200 years into the huge present-day city of Bangkok.

▲ The stupas of Ayutthaya once gleamed gold.

▼ Roots of a tree have grown around the broken head of a stone Buddha in the ruins of Ayutthaya.

▲ King Narai of Ayutthaya had a great curiosity and tried to learn about the advances of other countries. This drawing records the king and French priest-astronomers watching a solar eclipse in 1688.

▲ Sword-fighting, boxing, and other martial arts were taught in Ayutthaya.

TREATIES WITH THE WEST

In 1782 a new king, Rama I, claimed the throne of Siam. He was the first monarch of the Chakri Dynasty. Since then, nine Chakri kings have ruled through 200 years of change in trade, agriculture, government, and everyday life. This era of change began in Europe when the invention of steam-driven engines set the Industrial Revolution in motion. Steamships brought Europeans to Southeast Asia, where they competed for materials and landbases. Siam had two remarkable monarchs who were students of Western language and science: King Mongkut (1851–1868) and his son, King Chulalonghorn (1868–1910). They kept Siam free by negotiating treaties with Britain, the strongest European nation. Treaties with other countries followed, but Siam was the only Southeast Asian nation not colonized by European powers. However, the Siamese were eager to learn Western ways.

▲
Nine-tiered parasol, symbol of the Chakri Dynasty.

▲
King Mongkut, Rama IV, in traditional dress for his coronation.

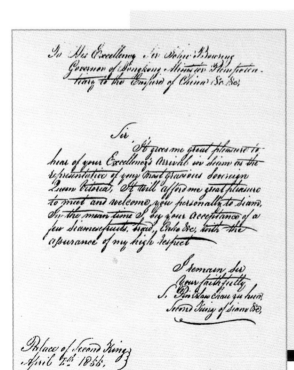

THE COMING OF BRITAIN AND WORLD TRADE

◄ British envoy, Sir John Bowring, arrived at Bangkok by steamship in 1855. As the ship lay anchored in the harbor, King Mongkut sent this letter to graciously welcome him. Taking steps to keep control of his country, the king entertained Sir John and signed the Bowring Treaty. Britain gained the right to harvest forest timber, to set up businesses, and to sell British goods free of tax. Siam gained British protection from other nations.

► Elephants were first trained to haul logs when Britain began to extract teak wood from Siam's forests in the 1880s.

◀ Princes playing *khlee* (polo). Ten players used long sticks to hit a wooden ball through goal posts.

▶ King Chulalonghorn's new palace was built in an Italian style, but with Siamese spires. A Thai joke calls it "a *farang* (foreigner) wearing a *chada*" (the headdress of a Thai classical dancer).

British large-scale projects, such as timber and rice production for sale on the world market, brought changes to villages. Before this, each village grew its own food, and women ground rice and wove cloth. Now, when men went to work for wages, the women had to do all the farm work and began to buy milled rice and factory-woven cloth from the government. The royal family and upper classes studied in Western universities but kept Thai culture.

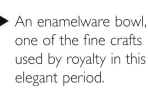

▶ An enamelware bowl, one of the fine crafts used by royalty in this elegant period.

▲ The royal children had European tutors or were sent to the best schools in England, France, Germany, and Russia to prepare them for service in modern Thailand.

◀ Men and boys soon preferred to dress in top hats and suits like the English.

▲ Queen to His Majesty, King Rama V, wearing traditional Thai *chong kraben* with a finely embroidered blouse in the European fashion of the time.

NEW WAYS, NEW ALLIES

Since its beginning in 1296, the nation of Siam had been ruled by an absolute monarchy (that is, kings had power to make all decisions). But by 1932, students returning from France wanted a modern government in which decisions would be made by an elected parliament. They joined with the military and noblemen, who wanted a place in the government, and together they overturned the king. A military government took control and made the king a constitutional monarch. His role was to bring people together under the new style of government. Democracy was not achieved, and since 1932, there have been many plots, revolutions, and constitutions with the army in power most of the time.

▲
Nobles, angry because the King appointed his relatives to high positions, joined students and the military to overturn the King.

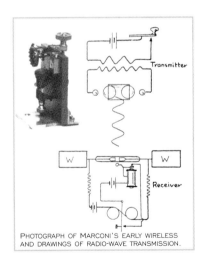

▲ The first heavier-than-air flying machine was seen in Bangkok in 1911. By 1927 Thailand had built its own bi-plane.

▼ The Great Depression of the 1930s caused low prices for produce on the world market. This meant cuts in the peasant farmers' wages and caused them great poverty.

PHOTOGRAPH OF MARCONI'S EARLY WIRELESS AND DRAWINGS OF RADIO-WAVE TRANSMISSION.

▲
Thailand's royal and upper classes were enthusiastic about European ideas and education. Schools taught English and Chinese as well as Thai. Uniforms and youth groups were also popular.

▲
Wireless (radio) was one of the new technologies from Europe quickly taken up by the Thais. The government used radio broadcasts to gain the people's support for its great changes.

▲ Monks before a golden Buddha. In the 1930s Buddhism was promoted as the state religion.

In 1939, to build a sense of national pride, the country's name was officially declared to be Thailand, not Siam. Also at this time, many Asians were encouraged by Japan's invasion of Russia and China—a small Asian nation had been stronger than the great powers that had dominated Asia for centuries. So when the Japanese Army swept over Southeast Asia in 1941, Thailand's prime minister felt sure they would win. He agreed to Japanese army bases in Thailand, but Japan's promises of liberation and "Asia for the Asians" proved false. Instead, they took over Thailand's food supplies, facilities, and labor to support the Japanese armies until World War II ended in 1945.

▶ The Japanese flag. World War II (1939–1945) began in Europe and spread to Southeast Asia when Japan declared war in the Pacific in 1941.

THAILAND-BURMA RAILWAY—WORLD WAR II

A railway line to carry supplies to the Japanese army in Burma was constructed through some of Thailand's most rugged mountains and jungle. This line was built by the forced labor of Asians and Allied forces prisoners-of-war, whose tools were picks, shovels, and hand-baskets. Japanese headquarters ordered that the line be built in one year (1942–1943), so prisoners were forced to work until many died from starvation and exhaustion. Monsoon rains turned camps into disease-ridden mud, adding to deaths. At war's end, 240,000 Asians had disappeared and 13,000 prisoners-of-war had died.

▲ Prisoners constructing a railway bridge, drawn with ink and brush by M. Griffin.

▶ Asian women loading drums of petrol onto a supply train.

WAR AND PEACE

After World War II ended in 1945, Thailand was in the center of one of the world's major trouble-spots: the defeated Japanese had to be sent home; the countries they had occupied were trying to return to normal; everything was disrupted and help was needed. But from where would this help come? Europe was also struggling to recover from the war, and in any case, Asians did not want the Europeans to move back. Communist Russia and China now wanted to take control of Southeast Asia. The United States and other Western powers tried to prevent this. Finally the tension between the Communists and the West exploded into a destructive war in Vietnam (1957–1973). Thailand, now allied with the United States, became a base for 50,000 American troops. Later (1975–1980), Cambodia and Laos suffered war and persecution as Communists and dictators fought for power. Those who escaped became homeless refugees and many sought asylum in Thailand.

▲

Leaders in the West feared that communism would capture the Southeast Asian countries one after the other, like a row of falling dominoes (called the Domino Theory). To try to prevent Vietnam falling to the Communists, the United States joined the war in Vietnam.

▶

During the 1970s, hundreds of thousands of refugees fled from Cambodia and Laos into Thailand. Driven from their own countries by dictators, wars, and famine, they streamed into camps set up on Thailand's borders. Finding food and shelter for so many was a mammoth problem, and Thailand asked for help from world aid organizations.

Following the war in Vietnam the Southeast Asian countries formed two blocs: those eager to have new technology and open trade like the Western countries—and those who chose to join China and the Soviet Union under closed communist governments. But by 1990 the countries were working to heal divisions and work cooperatively.

▶ King Bhumibol and Queen Sirikit in front of the nine-tiered Chakri parasol. They were married and crowned in 1950, promising, "We will reign with righteousness for the benefit and happiness of the Siamese people." They are everywhere honored for having kept their promise.

◀ Jim Thompson's teakwood house and Thai Silk Company are now well-known. In 1945 he was sent to Thailand on a secret mission for U.S. intelligence.

▼ After the war he remained to sell the beautiful Thai silk to the west, where it soon became a prized dress fabric.

▲ Khao Yai, the first National Park in Thailand, was created in 1961. For exotic birds, such as the hornbill, it is a perfect habitat.

▼ American entertainments introduced by troops based in Thailand included movies. . .

▼ . . . mechanical fun-rides and amusement parks such as Bangkok's Yo-Yo Land. . .

▼ . . . fast-food eating-places and big, bright advertising, like this mock plane crashing into a building.

GOVERNING THE KINGDOM

Thailand's government describes itself as "moving toward democracy." Since 1932, Parliamentary organization has been somewhat like the British Westminster system with a prime minister, but election of a government by democratic vote has been hard to achieve. The present government is the most stable yet. The constitution sets out the rights and freedoms of the people, but these rights and freedoms are not to be used against "the Nation, religion, the King, and the Constitution."

▲ The Royal emblem.

◀ The Council of Ministers meets in Parliament house under the leadership of the prime minister. The king, as head of state, is not involved in decision-making. But his support is important, and several times, in national crisis, he has saved the country from disruption.

▲ Buddhism is the state religion, but under the Thai constitution, people are free to follow their chosen religion, to speak or print their opinions, and to meet in groups.

▲ The prow of the King's barge, one of the historic treasures maintained for ceremonial occasions.

▲ King Bhumibol, with his daughter taking notes, talks to local people.

THE KING AND QUEEN

King Bhumibol and Queen Sirikit have made close contact with the people by traveling to every region to see and discuss their problems. The king's projects have improved life for rural people (see page 31, "New Theory") and health, education and environment for all. One of the queen's successes has been the revival of traditional crafts.

▶ The queen encourages village silk weavers.

Thailand's modern national flag was introduced in 1917. The blue band stands for the king, red for the nation, and white for religion.

▲ The Thai government seeks to work with other nations on such joint matters as bird sanctuaries and protection of ocean fishing grounds.

► Communications technology is encouraged.

▲ ▶
People can earn through their own efforts whether they run large international companies which import and export goods or small businesses, such as family umbrella-makers.

▲ Police keep order in towns.

◀ The efficient and powerful army protects the country's borders. It has also often controlled the government.

▼ Citizens are free to move about in their country wherever they wish.

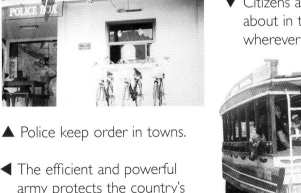

THAILAND AND THE WORLD

Thais have a long history of adapting ideas from other countries to their own culture. From ancient times they absorbed the religions and architecture of India; in the eighteenth century, foreign traders exchanged exotic goods in Ayutthaya; nineteenth-century King Chulalonghorn studied European science, English language, and literature; in the early twentieth century the Thais began to organize their government along democratic principles and to wear Western clothing. Now in the twenty-first century, the Thais work in partnership with leading world manufacturers and apply modern agricultural science to farming. Thailand has avoided major wars in its land, but makes foreign businesses and tourists welcome. And it is easy to see and enjoy the natural beauty and traditional arts and crafts of Thailand.

▲ Musical notation was introduced through Western classical music. Before this, Thai instruments and music were played by memory.

▼ A symphony orchestra plays European music with a backdrop of Thai art.

▶ Thailand has set aside national parks and wildlife sanctuaries to preserve its World Heritage forests. But, of course, the areas cannot be large enough to feed the herds of large animals which once roamed the whole peninsula. People are also trying new ways to grow enough food by natural methods.

▼ Coins of the world are being collected on Thai Airways flights to help protect Asia's environment.

▲ Orchids are flown to Tokyo every day.

◄ Dolls such as this are often presented to official visitors from foreign countries.

► The Chinese New Year is celebrated with dragon and lion dances. In Nakhon Sawan seven nations take part in the festivities.

▲ Food being distributed to refugees from Cambodia and Laos. Other countries also assist with supplies and aid-workers.

◄ Pigeons roost on buildings and fly up from city parks in Thailand as they do in cities across the world.

▼ Silks are exported in every color and in a multitude of woven patterns.

◄ Sunthon Phu, a classical poet honored by Thais, is also recognized by UNESCO (United Nations Educational, Scientific, and Cultural Organization).

FISH IN THE RIVER, RICE IN THE FIELD

With rich land and plentiful water, Thailand is largely an agricultural country. The seven major crops are: rice, tapioca, rubber, maize, sugarcane, mung beans, and tobacco leaves. Most of these crops are grown for export. In areas where water is controlled, farmers can grow two crops in a year, but more than half the farmlands have no water control and many crops are damaged by age-old problems of flooding during the monsoonal wet season, or drought during the dry summer. New technology is now improving the quality of dairy foods (milk, butter, cream) and livestock (beef, pork, and poultry). The government has restricted log-cutting in depleted forests while reforestation is carried out.

▲ Most fish are caught from the sea, but freshwater fish farms are also being set up.

▲ Four pigs are riding to market in two woven baskets!

◀ Galangal, basil, and chillis are some of the herbs grown. Others are lemon grass, shallots, and tamarind.

▼ Rock salt deposits are estimated to contain two billion tons of pure salt.

Orchid farms ▼ export to Japan, the U.S., and Europe.

Beef, pork, and dairy animals need large farm areas and good water supplies.

Because of their ability to adapt, Thai farmers have been able to grow crops to sell on changing markets. The king has visited all regions to see what the people need to improve their lives. Hill farmers are learning how to farm organically, without pesticides or chemical fertilizers. Their high quality vegetables are used as organic meals on international airlines.

▲

Macaque monkeys, trained to work for their living, can pick up to 1,000 coconuts a day from coco palms.

▼ ▶

Rice, a leading export crop, is grown in the fertile plains of the Chao Phraya River and transported downriver to the seaport to be shipped to market.

NEW THEORY

One of the king's most important projects, the "New Theory" approach to land and water management on small farms, helps poorer farmers become self-sufficient.

Phase one aims for each household to produce enough rice for its own use for the whole year. To do this there must be enough water to carry through the dry season. Reservoirs are built to supply water to each farmer's pond.

The government assists by digging farm ponds, giving technical advice, and supplying fish for the ponds.

In later phases, farmers are encouraged to work co-operatively and then to find markets for their produce.

EACH FARM OF SIX ACRES IS DIVIDED INTO FOUR PARTS:

- 30% for a water storage pond
- 30% for rice-planting in the rainy season
- 30% for fruit and field crops for use or market
- 10% for housing, animals, and farming.

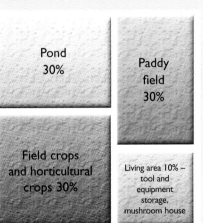

Pond 30%

Paddy field 30%

Field crops and horticultural crops 30%

Living area 10% – tool and equipment storage, mushroom house

▲

Small backyard gardens supply daily foods, such as fresh vegetables, fruit, and rabbits.

▲

Farmers can work in their fields even during rain when they have a water control system.

THAILAND

1997 1998

1999 2000

INVEST NOW

▲ Poster shows Thailand's economic progress from 1997 to 2000.

▲ Cutting, polishing, and making
▼ the gems into jewelry are important industrial crafts.

INDUSTRY AND TRADE

Thailand has many small and medium-sized enterprises that supply parts for large manufacturing companies, including Ford, Mitsubishi and Toyota. To learn exactly what is needed small companies visit the large factories. Thailand trades with other members of ASEAN (Association of South East Asian Nations) and also welcomes foreign companies who wish to set up business. The main products are shown in the graphs below.

▶

Thailand's top ten imports do not include food. Most imports are used to produce goods to resell.

▶

In this graph of Thailand's most important export industries, you can see that the sale of computer parts earns the most.

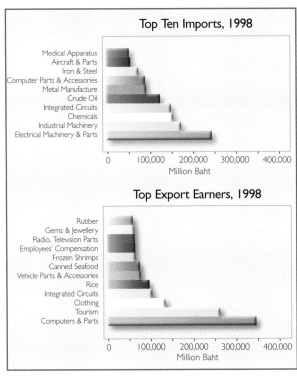

Top Ten Imports, 1998

Medical Apparatus
Aircraft & Parts
Iron & Steel
Computer Parts & Accessories
Metal Manufacture
Crude Oil
Integrated Circuits
Chemicals
Industrial Machinery
Electrical Machinery & Parts

0   100,000   200,000   300,000   400,000
Million Baht

Top Export Earners, 1998

Rubber
Gems & Jewellery
Radio, Television Parts
Employees' Compensation
Frozen Shrimps
Canned Seafood
Vehicle Parts & Accessories
Rice
Integrated Circuits
Clothing
Tourism
Computers & Parts

0   100,000   200,000   300,000   400,000
Million Baht

▼ Thai factories engineer and assemble parts for heavy industry, such as airplanes.

▲ Sapphires and other precious stones are mined in Thailand's north.

▲ Garments are made for local and overseas markets. (See graph, page 32).

▲ Important small businesses include: forging, engineering plastics, cutting and grinding tools, antilock braking systems, and electronic fuel injection systems.

▼ Exported foods include coconut milk, fish sauce, mangos, and curry paste.

TECHNOLOGY AND TOURISM

Air, rail, and road transport provided by technology is used by up to 8 million tourists a year. The government has assisted tourism by creating hotels, resorts, historic parks, eco-tours, and information services. This provides work for many people and export income for Thailand.

▲ Automation moves luggage quickly.

◄ Tourist resorts provide luxuries such as beauty salons and health diet meals.

▶ Eco-tourism allows visitors to see the natural beauty of the country without damaging it.

BANGKOK–KRUNG THEP

The world knows Thailand's huge chaotic capital as Bangkok, but Thais call their city *Krung Thep*,* "City of Angels." Built on Thailand's great river, the Chao Phraya, Bangkok is forty times bigger than any other Thai city: the King's Palace and Parliament buildings are there; it is the center of culture, government, and trade; the most important museums, universities, and factories are there. Bangkok is Thailand's point of contact with the world and a leading Asian business center. Activity surrounds the temples and gold spires of the old city, begun by King Rama I in 1782.

◀ Giant guards at the Royal Palace.

▶ Many canals that once drained Bangkok have been filled in, causing the city to flood and slowly sink.

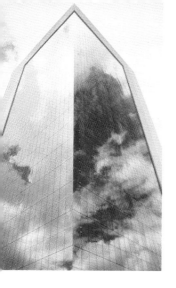

▲ Head office tower of Thai Airways.

Fly-over expressways and concrete highrise business centers were built in the last thirty years. Beyond them are stylish emporiums, factories, and warehouses; dark laneways overflowing with open stalls; rows of newer apartments; and the poor, crowded slum shelters of rural workers come to seek better pay, but hardly surviving.

▶ Fashion goods are sold in emporiums.

▲▶ Mammoth traffic jams and the worst air pollution in the world make daily life difficult for the city's six million people, but they accept this as part of modern life and higher wages.

▲ Bank notes. Unit of currency is the Baht.

▼ Traditional Thai houses made entirely of teak wood panels could be dismantled, transported by boat, and easily reerected. Set on stilts, they are air-cooled.

▲ Bangkok is famous for its food and international restaurants.

▲ The queen wearing Thai silk *pha sin*, the traditional skirt, for a state occasion.

BEING THAI

Some of the light-hearted things Thais love are color and spectacle, brightly decorated processions and ceremonies, games, and fun (*sanuk*). They often use the greeting, *"Pai nai?"* It means "Where are you going?" or just "hello." The answer is often *"Pai thiaw"*—"I'm out having fun." Rather than show anger, an easy-going Thai person will smile and say, *"Mai pen rai"*—"It doesn't matter . . . no problem." Thais also love anything new or technological, and they have a serious side that respects parents, king, country, and religion.

▶ Water and boats have always been part of life in Thailand. Produce is sold at canal boat-markets and transported on river barges and seagoing carriers.

▶ At special times of the year, Thai monks dress the massive statues of Buddha in saffron yellow.

▼ Triangular cushions are a Thai craft.

▶ Mural painting is a favorite Thai art that shows royal events and daily life of the past.

▼ *Takraw* is a favorite Thai game in which a rattan ball is kept in the air without using the hands.

◀ Being Thai is sharing a joke while waiting for a ferry.

▶ . . . kindly letting your cat enjoy a warm spot on a banana stall.

▼ . . . or embroidering a purse.

▶ Racing water buffalo and getting very wet and very muddy is a once-a-year Thai sport, held after harvest.

FAMILY AND FRIENDS

Traditional village life suits the sociable nature of the Thai people. Families and neighbors, who are often related, gather to chat or take part in community events. Crowded city life still pauses to enjoy a parade or holiday, but it is impossible to keep the close community of the village. Ties with extended family, such as uncles or cousins, have a strong effect on public life, because leaders often feel they must appoint their relatives to official positions. Young children do not usually have lots of toys but love games and, like everyone else, they are part of the group and learn to get along with people of all ages.

▲ Meals cooked by Mother or Grandmother begin with a trip to the market.

◄ Women do much of the work and often manage the family's money.

◄ Most villagers take an interest in all the children. While older children go to school, younger ones play near parents or neighbors.

▲ Families prepare enough food to provide early-morning alms (offerings) to the Buddhist monks who go about the streets and canals to collect their daily rations.

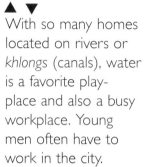

▲ ▼
With so many homes located on rivers or *khlongs* (canals), water is a favorite play-place and also a busy workplace. Young men often have to work in the city.

▲ In villages, the temple and markets are important.

▲ "Hold hands like this."

▶ "That's right."

▼ Health care for children is a major concern. The tropical climate means that cuts easily become infected, mosquitoes carry malaria, and skin diseases are severe.

◀ Babies everywhere love to go with older brothers or sisters.

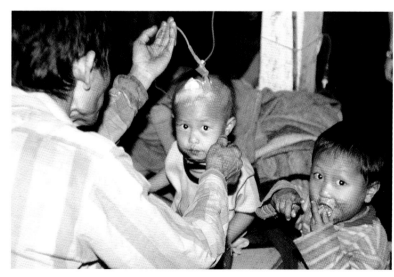

EATING THAI

Thai chefs say, "Cook till you smell the spices." Hot, spicy curries, meat, fish, and vegetables are served with side dishes and rice or noodles. Snacks are very popular, and vendors sell tiny sweets, such as pancakes and sticky rice in banana leaves, and freshly squeezed fruit juice, sugarcane juice, and coconut milk.

▲
Grinding spices with a mortar and pestle. Red pepper is a favorite.

◀ ▼ ▶
At the markets there are lots of green vegetables and fresh fruit. Seafood, meat, and even frogs are prepared ready to cook.

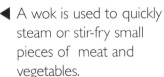

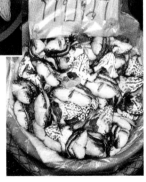

▼
Chiang Mai stalls sell a thick, spicy sausage made from minced pork, rice and garlic.

◀ A wok is used to quickly steam or stir-fry small pieces of meat and vegetables.

▼ Rain is caught in water pots for cooking; for drinking, bottled water is sold everywhere.

In Thailand people will travel long distances to enjoy the special dishes of different regions. Overseas, many people like to gather with friends to "eat Thai." Some travel to Thailand to learn how to cook the tasty and healthy traditional dishes.

▶
Shrimp (or prawn) platters are one of the delicacies for festive meals.

▲
This woman is learning Thai cookery in a class where students live in the teacher's home and prepare the meals.

HOW TO EAT THAI

- A plate of boiled rice, a fork, and a spoon (or chopsticks for noodles) are placed before each person. Order several different kinds of food to share.
- All dishes are served at once with side dishes for dipping. Take only one or two spoonfuls from a serving dish. After eating this portion, try another.
- In the left hand use the fork to put food on the spoon, then eat from the spoon (food is in bite-sized pieces so no knife is needed).
- Sticky rice is taken in the fingers of the right hand (never the left, which is used for washing the body).

◀ Royal Thai, once prepared only by royal chefs, comes to the table in enamelware bowls.

◀ Quick snacks can be dried squid barbecued over coals

▼ . . . or a canal-side meal served from a mobile kitchen.

▲
A meal is often finished with fresh fruit.

LEARNING

The Thai government aims to provide education for all citizens: the school program has six years at primary level, three in lower secondary and three in upper secondary. All schools use the same curriculum. There are more than forty universities and teachers' colleges. Courses are also offered to adults and people with special needs, such as the handicapped or unemployed and those who have not been able to attend school or learn vocational skills.

Every Thai school child is taught to memorize King Ramkhamhaeng's first work of Thai literature, which begins *"Naam mii plaa, nai naa mii khao"* or "In the water there are fish, in the fields there is rice."

◀ Children who live on the network of rivers and canals catch the "school boat." Those on roads catch buses.

▼ Technology and machine-operating skills are taught.

◀ Children are immunized against infectious diseases.

▼ It is compulsory to attend primary school for six years.

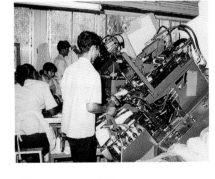

▼ Practical skills to help young people find employment include gardening.

▲ By interviewing travelers, senior school girls improve their English language, which is important for international careers.

Universities train scientists, engineers, and economists for industry and agro-industry (where farm produce is grown and also processed or packed ready to sell). Others specialize in technology, commerce, or building.

MONASTERY SCHOOLS

Before government education began in 1961, most schools were in Buddhist monasteries. Many boys still leave their parents and family and live in a monastery. Monks teach them about Buddhism as well as school subjects. There are strict rules, and the boys help with work such as sweeping. Each day people give them a portion of food (this gift is believed to earn merit for the giver). Many boys remain only a few months, others for all of their schooling. Poor boys can get an education in this way, but the king also studied in a monastery for many years.

▶

A procession for fourteen-year-old boys who are about to become novice monks. They are dressed to represent the Indian Prince Siddhartha before he left his palace and family to seek meaning in his life. Later, people began to call him the Buddha.

▼

A monk has only eight basic belongings: three robes (long pieces of saffron yellow cotton), a girdle to tie the robe, an alms bowl in which daily food is collected, a razor to shave the head, a needle, and a water-strainer.

▶ These engineers represent the many university graduates.

▶
At home and in mosque schools Muslim children are taught to read their Holy Book, the Koran and to pray five times daily.

VISITING THAILAND

Thai people are used to welcoming visitors—up to eight million fly into their country each year! Most visits begin in the noisy streets and exotic palaces and temples of Bangkok, but 90 percent of the population live in farmlands or remote mountain villages. There you can see local crafts, processions, and festivals. But in this beautiful land, you could spend a whole vacation enjoying the forests, waterfalls and rivers, beaches, and islands.

◀ In the south, at Krabi, sea eagles and swiftlets nest in caves and islands of eroded limestone.

▲ Hand-painted paper parasols

▼ . . . and palm-leaf "mushrooms" are for sun—not rain!

DRESS IMPOLITE CAN'T ENTER THIS TEMPLE

SOME THAI CULTURAL NOTES

- As the sign above says, "impolite" dress is not allowed in a temple. Tourist guides recommend long trousers or skirts and covered arms.
- Many rituals are performed and each action has a spiritual meaning. If you do not know what a ritual is about, do not take part, but be courteous to believers.
- Never speak ill of the king or his family. He is revered by Thais and the law protects him from criticism.
- Stand still when the king's anthem or the national anthem is played (at 8 a.m. and 6 p.m. in public places, such as parks, railway stations, and cinemas).

▲ A Phu Thai welcoming ceremony, in which a group joins with a witch doctor in performing a sacrificial ritual.

▶ The Thai way of saying hello or goodbye is the *wei*, a slight bow with fingertips together.

▲
In Bangkok, visit the fabulous Royal Palace. The ornate buildings have steps with lions and other fierce creatures, ornate doors patterned with colored tiles, and fanciful gilded statues.

▶ Try some sweets. These are colored and molded in fruit shapes.

◀
Sleep in a thatched bungalow in the mountains.

▶
Northern hill tribe children will find you interesting.

▼ Don't forget elephant bath-time!

INDEX

PICTURE CREDITS

Abbreviations: r = right, l = left,
t = top, c = center, b = below

Tourism Authority of Thailand
8 tl, cl, br; **9** br; **10** tl, bl; **11** cr; **12** cr, bl; **13** tr, cr, br; **15** tl; **16** b; **17** tr, bl, br; **18** tl, b; **19** br; **20** br; **21** tl; **23** tl; **25** cl, bl, bc, br; **26** tr, cl; **27** tr; **28** cl, br; **29** bl; **30** bl; **31** tl, tr, bct, brt; **32** cl, bl, bc; **33** cb, ct, bc, br; **34** t, br; **35** tr, cr, bl; **36** c, br; **37** tr, bl; **38** cr; **43** cr; **44** cr, bl, br; **45** b.

Margaret Sams
Contents; **11** cl; **13** bl; **14** tl, cr, bl; **21**tr; **25** crt; **27** bc, br; **28** c, cr; **30** tr br; **31** bcb, brb; **34** bl; **35** clt, br; **37** cl, cr, br; **38** tr, bl; **39** tl, trc, cl, crt, crb; **40** tl, clt, clb, c, bl, br; **41** cl, bl,

bc; **42** c; **43** tl; **44** cl; **45** tl, tr, cr.

Royal Thai Consulate
12 bl; **13** cl, cl, c; **15** tr; **17** cl, cr; **20** tl, tr; **21** cl, cr, bc; **22** tr, cl, ct, br; **25** tr; **26** bc, br; **29** br; **31** bl; **32** tl; **33** cl; **36** tl, bl; **37** tl; **42** br; **43** tr, bl, br.
Statistics: **31** bl, **32** cr

Thai Airways International
Intoduction; **11** bc, br; **12** tl; **21** c; **25** crb; **26** cr, bl; **27** c; **29** tl, tr, bc; **30** c, cr; **32** br; **33** tl, tr, cr; **35** tl; **38** cl; **41** tr, c, br; **44** tl.

Peter Barker
9 map; **10** map; **11** tl; **12** cr; **15** map; **17** tl; **32** cr.

Samsam
24 br; **27** bl; **29** cl; **39** bl, br; **42** tr.

Christa Sams
Title; **19** tr, bl; **45** c.

Wayne Morton
42 cl, cr, bl.

Australian War Memorial Museum
23 bl, br.

David Jones
24 tl, **28** tl.

Allen Roberts
16 tl.

Bibliotheque Francais
19 bc.

Oxford University Press
20 bl.

Vineyard
8 bl; **11** tr, c; **19** tl; **30** c; **31** cr; **33** bl.

Every effort has been made to consult all relevant people and organizations. Any omissions or errors are unintentional and should be reported to Vineyard Freepress Pty Ltd.

Artwork:
23 bl. Griffin, Murray *Prisoners Constructing A Railway Bridge*, c.1945 Brush and Brown Ink and Wash Over Pencil 48.7 x 35.4 cm Australian War Memorial Art 25106
23 br. Australian War Memorial Negative/Art Number P00406.037